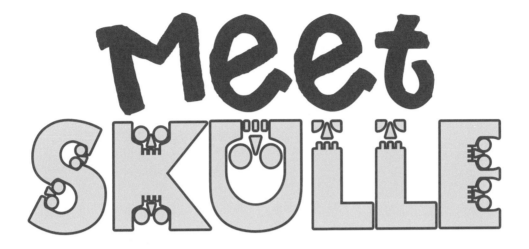

Meet SKULLE

Written by

Paulette Smartmackey

Illustrated by

Bruno Riberon

AuthorHouse™
1663 Liberty Drive
Bloomington, IN 47403
www.authorhouse.com
Phone: 833-262-8899

Because of the dynamic nature of the Internet, any web addresses or links contained in this book may have changed since publication and may no longer be valid. The views expressed in this work are solely those of the author and do not necessarily reflect the views of the publisher, and the publisher hereby disclaims any responsibility for them.

Any people depicted in stock imagery provided by Getty Images are models, and such images are being used for illustrative purposes only. Certain stock imagery © Getty Images.

This book is printed on acid-free paper.

ISBN: 978-1-6655-6070-2 (sc)
ISBN: 978-1-6655-6069-6 (e)

Library of Congress Control Number: 2022909575

Print information available on the last page.

Published by AuthorHouse 06/30/2023

authorHOUSE®

ACKNOWLEDGEMENT

Thanks to the Navigator
students and teachers for
giving Skulle an audience.

ACKNOWLEDGEMENTS

Thanks to my family for their
suggestions and listening ears.

Thanks to my namesake niece
for her proofreading tips.

Thanks to the AuthorHouse team
for their editing and publishing expertise.

Thanks to my artist for giving
Skulle some groovy moves.

To my sweet daughter, who is Skulle's inventor and first student.

To all the science explorers who are reading this book.

May your quest for knowledge spiral you to great heights.

I dedicate this book to you.

Hi, I'm Skulle. I'm a skeleton and your guide.

Welcome to the Science Center for Curious Kids.

Today's mission is to name my bones.

Then you can watch me make some dashing moves.

My body has many bones to help me move.

I can swim, jump, run, and do fun things
with my bones, as you name them.

Without bones, I would be floppy like a beach towel!

With bones, I can sit, stand, run, and do fun stuff like play the piano.

Bones are also a place for muscles to attach, and they protect essential organs like the heart and lungs.

There are bones everywhere in my body, and they are all connected.

The bones in my head are linked to my neck bones, which are connected to my backbone.

The bones in my back attach to my chest and hips.

The bones in my chest link to my arms, hands, and fingers.

And the hip bones connect to my thighs, legs, feet, and toes.

I can run, skate, jump, and play when all my bones are connected.

Watch me use my bones to skate!

Are you ready to start your mission?

Can you name this bone?

It's the bone that protects my brain.

It's where you find my eyes, nose, and ears.

Which bone is it?

SKULL

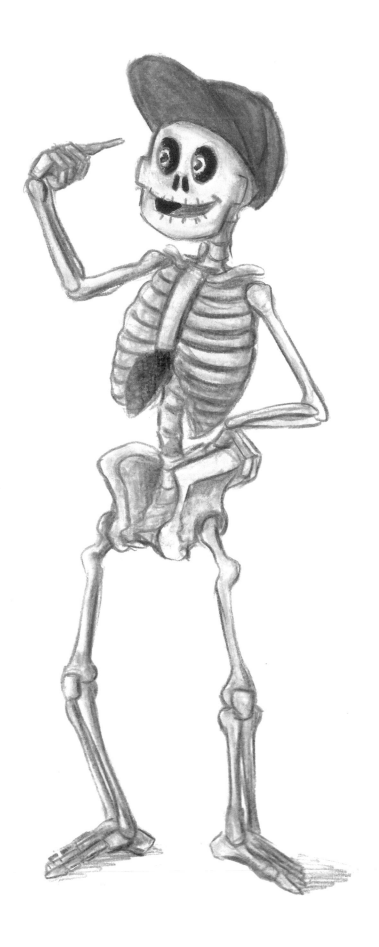

Did you guess the skull?

My brain lives inside the skull.

If I didn't have a skull, my brain would be out in the breeze.

Eww!

This bone is part of the face, and it helps me eat.

Without this bone, food would fall from my mouth.

Which bone is it?

MANDIBLE

If you guessed the mandible, then you're correct!

The mandible is the jawbone.

It moves up and down to help me chew foods like juicy apples.

Can you name this bone?

It's a bone that runs up and down my back.

Without it, I would topple over when I sit on the floor.

SPINE

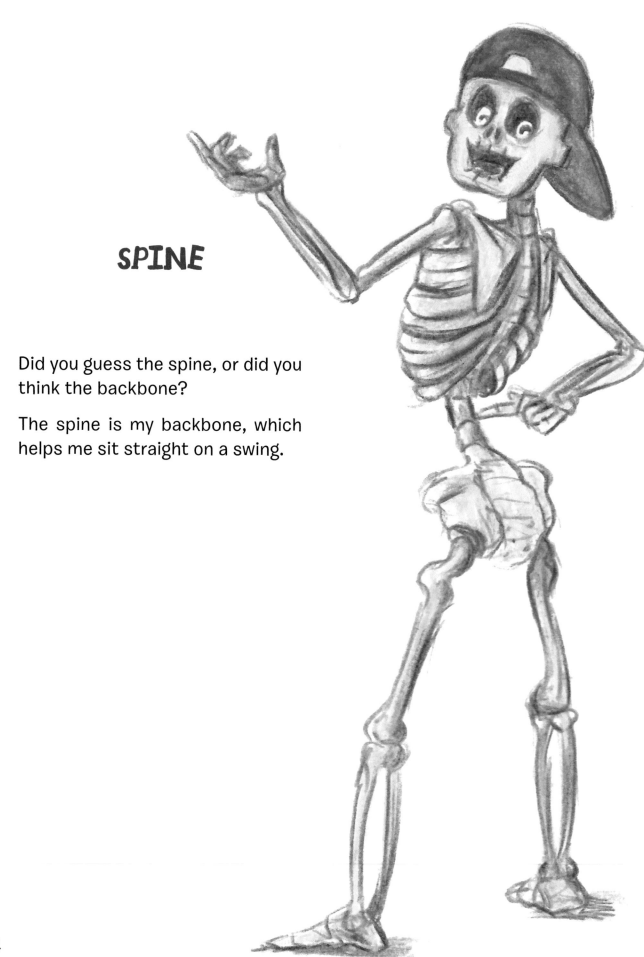

Did you guess the spine, or did you think the backbone?

The spine is my backbone, which helps me sit straight on a swing.

There are thirty-three bones in the spine, and each one is called a vertebra.

There are seven bones in the neck called cervical vertebrae.

There are twelve bones in the upper back called thoracic vertebrae.

There are five lower backbones called lumbar vertebrae.

The other vertebrae are fused to form the sacrum and coccyx.

I sit on my coccyx, which is my tailbone.

Did you know I have a tailbone?

The bones in my back stack together like pancakes with jelly in the middle!

There is jelly between each pair of vertebrae; this jelly is called a disc.

The discs cushion my vertebrae when I do activities.

Look at me swimming with my vertebrae in place!

Keep naming my bones,
and watch me use them to run.

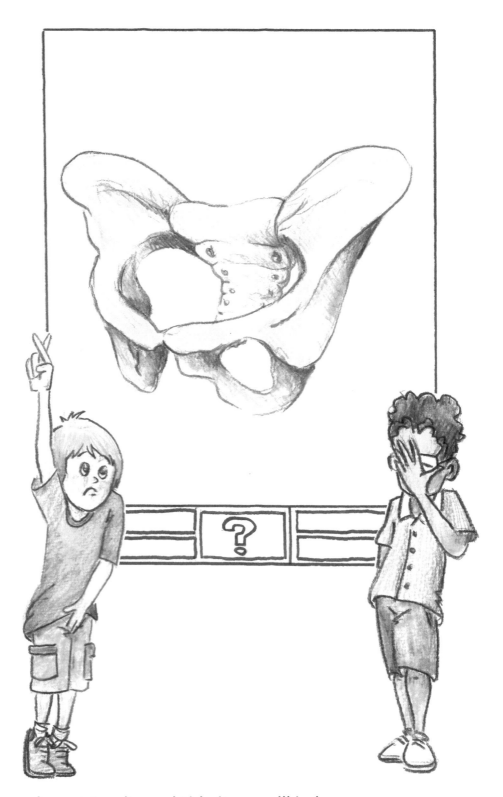

I want to sit, and this bone will help me.

It connects my back to my thighs.

Which bone is it?

PELVIS

The pelvis is the bone that helps me sit.

It connects my backbone to my thigh bones.

It's like a bucket without a handle, keeping

vital organs like the bladder safe.

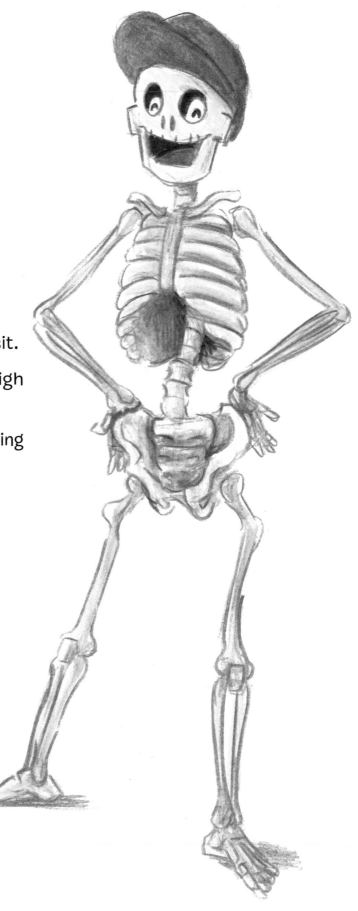

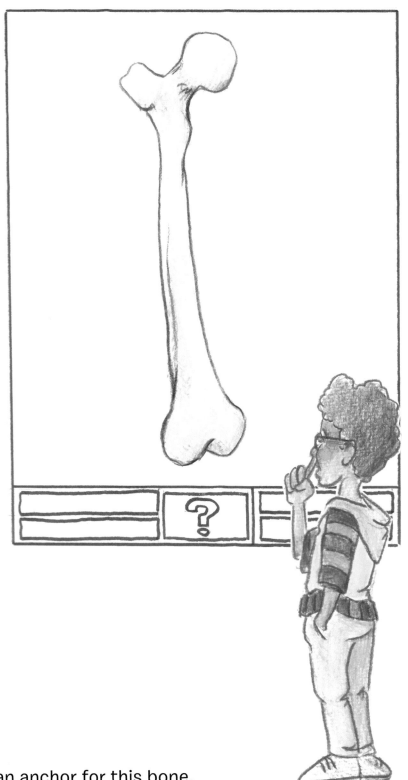

The pelvis is an anchor for this bone.

It helps me move my hips.

Which bone is it?

FEMUR

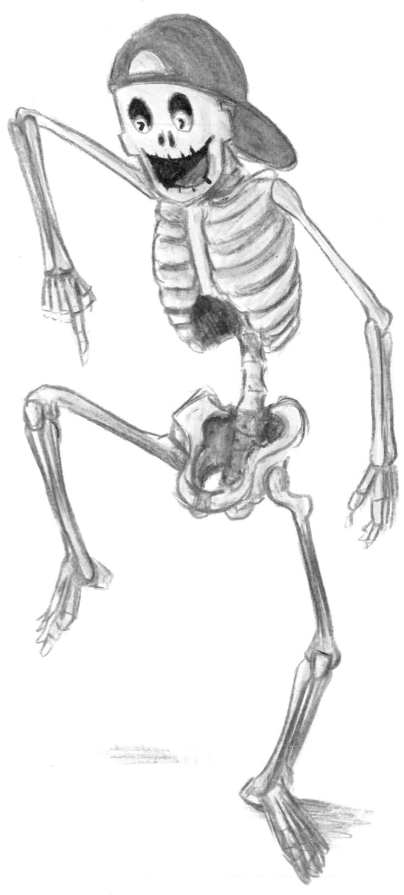

Did you say the femur?

The femur is my thigh bone.

I have one on the right side and another on the left.

They are my two longest bones, and they connect my knees to my hips.

Now I can run, kick, and play!

The thigh bone connects to two bones in my leg.

Can you guess their names?

TIBIA AND FIBULA

Yes! You guessed it!

The femur connects to two bones in my leg: the tibia and the fibula.

I call them Tib and Fib.

They run side by side from my knees to my ankles.

I have two sets of these bones, one set in each leg.

The tibia is the second longest bone in my body.

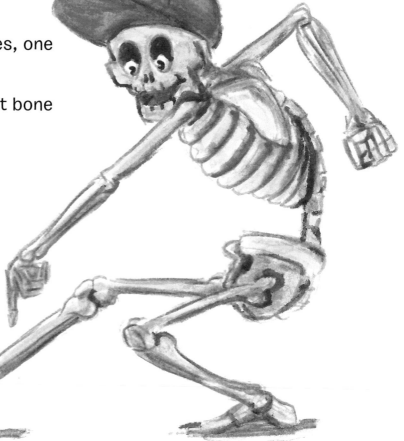

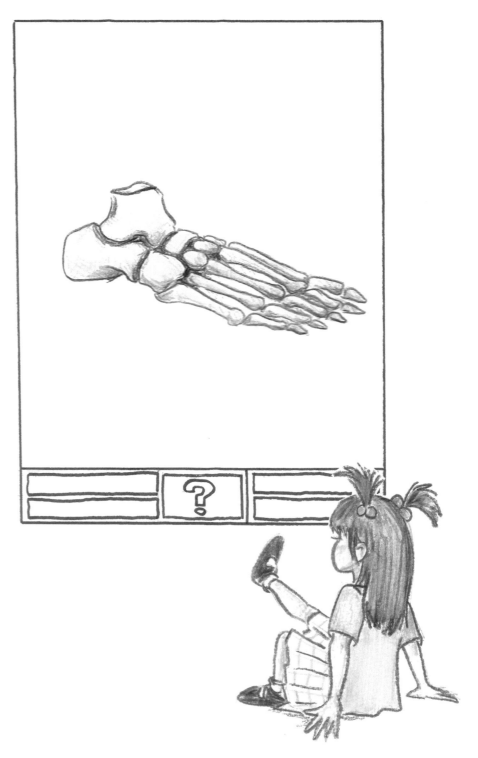

Now, let's name the bones in my feet.

I use them when I'm on my skateboard.

TARSALS, METATARSALS AND PHALANGES

The tarsals are the seven fancy bones in my ankle.

The metatarsals are the five spiffy bones in the middle of my feet.

And gee whiz! The phalanges are the many bones in my wiggly toes.

Great job naming my bones! Thank you!

Watch me use them to run, kick and play soccer!

Keep up the great work!

I have a few more bones for you to discover.

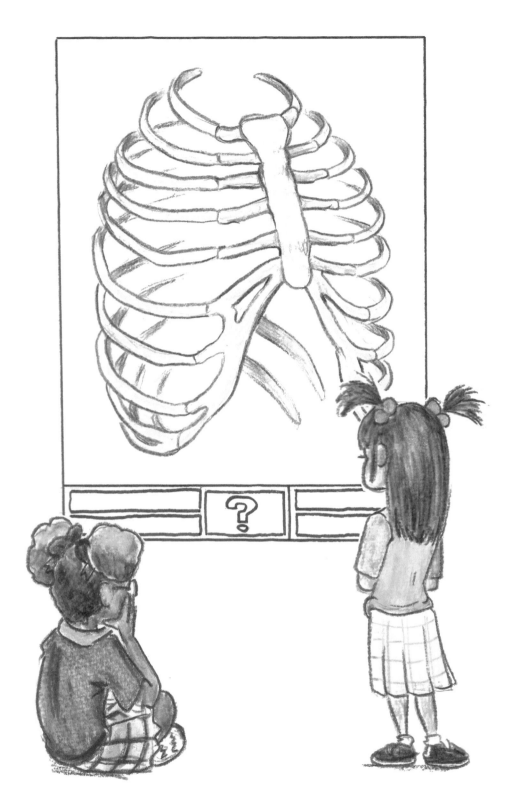

These bones help me breathe.

Can you guess the name?

RIB CAGE

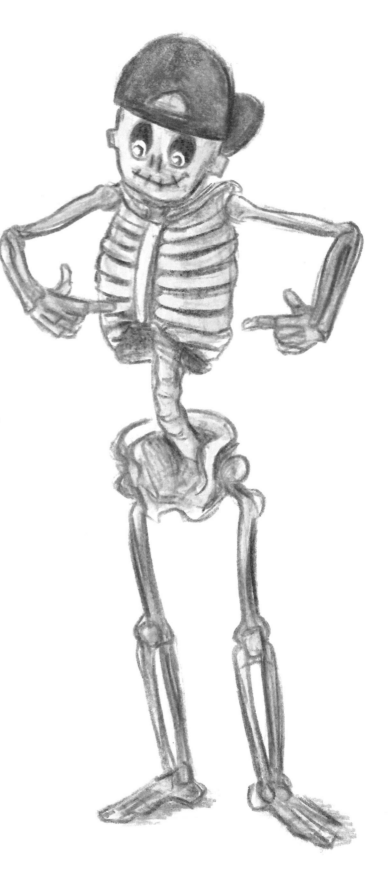

The set of bones that allows me to inhale and exhale is called the rib cage.

It moves up and down to help me take deep breaths.

The rib cage keeps my heart and lungs safe.

The cage forms when my ribs connect to my spine in the back and my breastplate in the front.

The breastplate is also called the sternum.

This bone goes from the top of my sternum to the top of my shoulder.

Can you name it? I have one on each side.

CLAVICLE

Did you guess the clavicle?

Cleaver Clavi is my collarbone.

The fancy name for collarbone is the clavicle.

You can feel your collarbone move when you raise your arm.

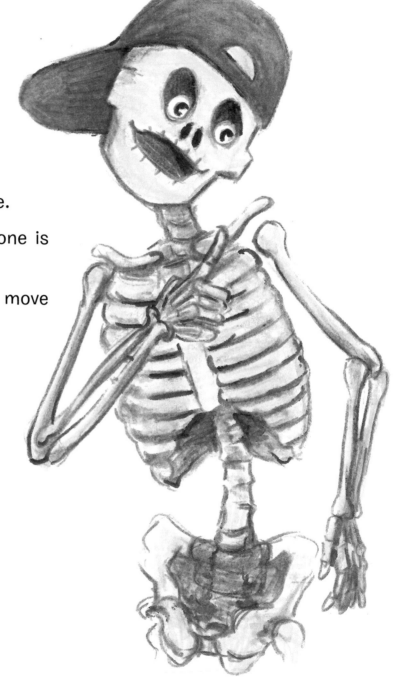

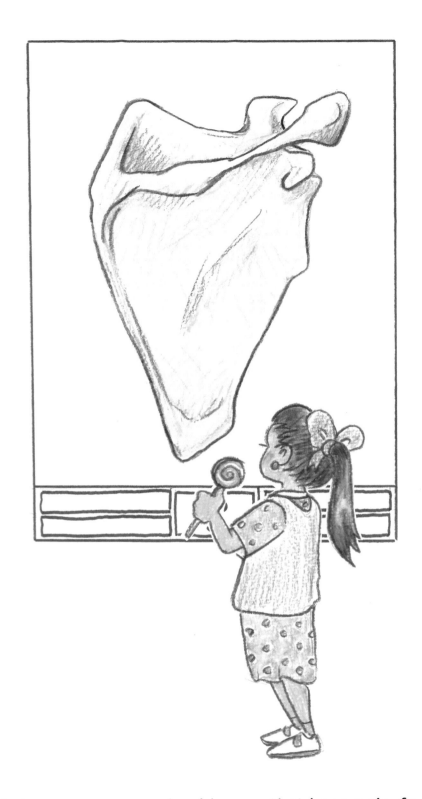

This bone helps me move my shoulders so that I can swim far and fast.

I have one on each side. Which bone is it?

SCAPULA

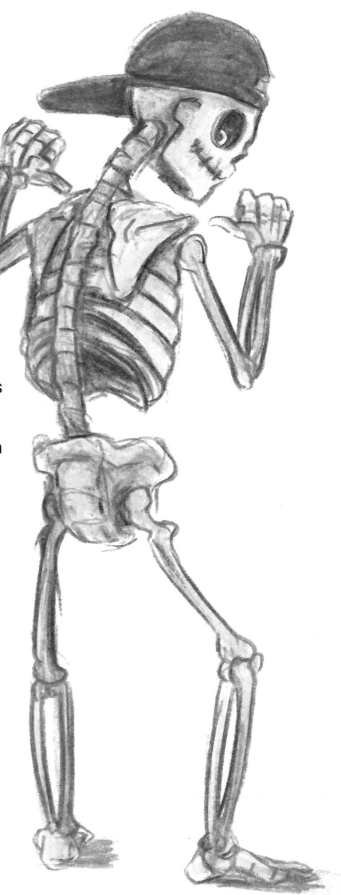

This bone is the scapula.

The scapula is my shoulder blade.

Muscles hold up my scapula, which is attached to the back of my rib cage.

It helps my shoulders move when I swim and row, row, row a boat.

The scapula also helps me throw
a basketball up high.

Watch me use my scapula to play ball!

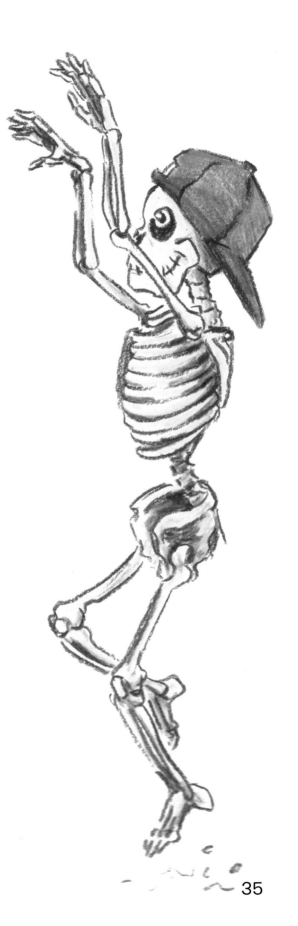

Excellent job naming my bones!

I have a few more bones left to identify, so let's keep going.

Labeling my bones gives me the energy to dash a hundred meters in a flash.

Now, let's take a look at my upper arm bone.

It moves when I raise my arm to touch my head.

Can you name this bone?

HUMERUS

This bone is the humerus

I call it the humor-me bone!

The humerus goes from my shoulder to my elbow.

I have two of them, one on my right side and one on my left.

My humerus holds a lot of muscles to help me lift that heavy box.

Now for the funny bones at my elbow that're not so funny.

The elbow is where you'll find these bones.

Can you guess their names?

RADIUS AND ULNA

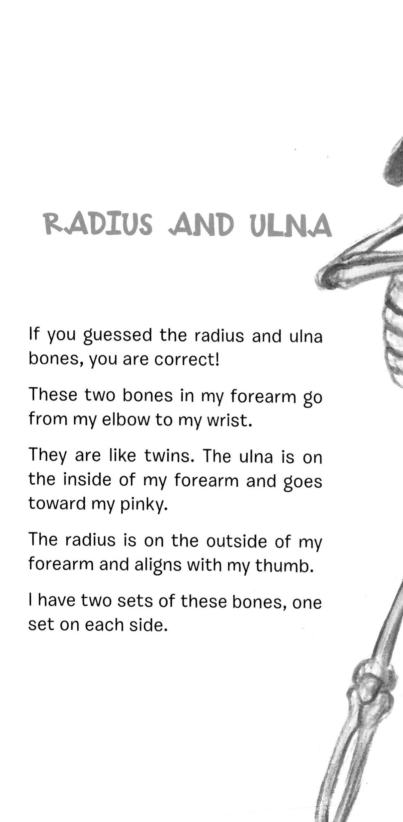

If you guessed the radius and ulna bones, you are correct!

These two bones in my forearm go from my elbow to my wrist.

They are like twins. The ulna is on the inside of my forearm and goes toward my pinky.

The radius is on the outside of my forearm and aligns with my thumb.

I have two sets of these bones, one set on each side.

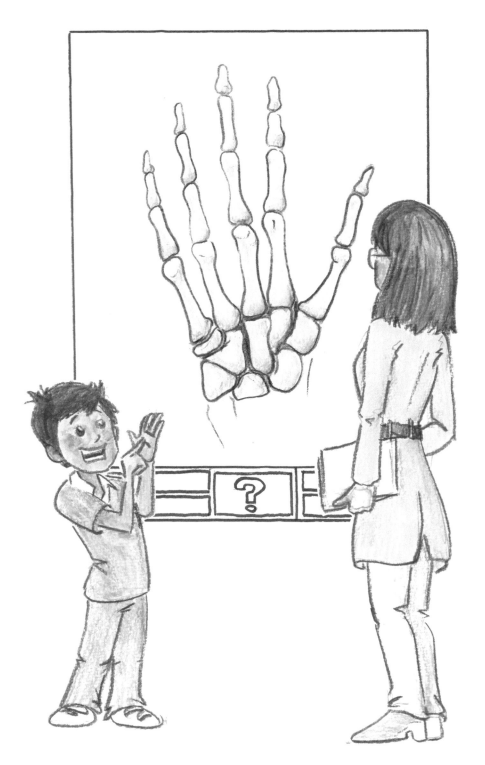

Wow! Look at my hand!

It has lots of bones.

Can you name them?

CARPALS, METACARPALS AND PHALANGES

Yes, like my feet, my hands have a lot of bones.

You can carpool down the arm to the carpals, which are the eight fancy bones in my wrist.

The metacarpals are the five bones in the middle of my hand, and you will find fourteen phalanges in my fingers and thumb.

The carpals, metacarpals, and phalanges work together to help me grasp things.

Now watch me use these bones to grasp these
sticks and raise my arms to drum up a beat!

Great work naming my arm,
forearm, and hand bones!

Watch me swing them back and
forth as I run!

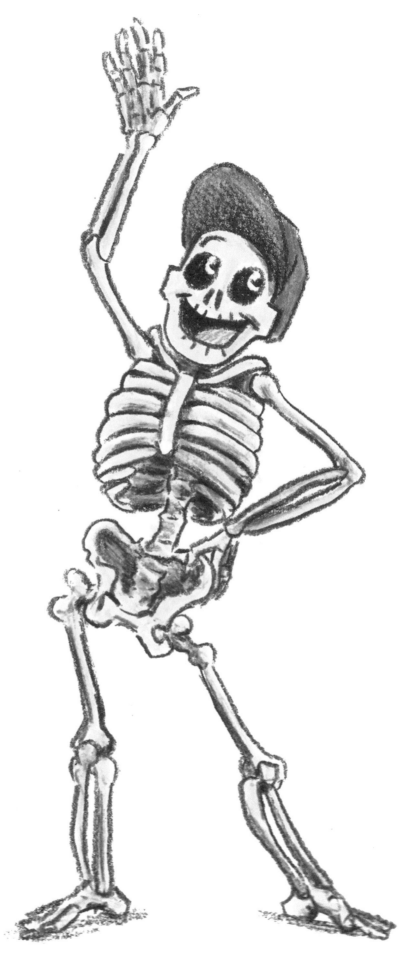

Thank you, my friends,
for helping to name all my bones.

Your mission is complete.

You are now an honorary
bone-naming scientist.

I can run, swing, jump, and
move about with these bones,
just like you.

I hope you enjoyed the mission to name my bones at the Science Center for Curious Kids.

Please come back soon to learn more about the human body.

Keep moving!

Printed in the United States
by Baker & Taylor Publisher Services